NATIVE AMERICAN HISTORIES

# THE CHOCTAWS

## BY LIZ SONNEBORN

CONSULTANT: JOE WATKINS, PH.D., RPA, ASSOCIATE PROFESSOR,
DEPARTMENT OF ANTHROPOLOGY, UNIVERSITY OF NEW MEXICO,
CHOCTAW TRIBAL MEMBER, TRIBAL CONSULTATION SPECIALIST

LERNER PUBLICATIONS COMPANY
MINNEAPOLIS

ABOUT THE COVER IMAGE: This Choctaw basket of woven split cane is decorated with geometric shapes. Draped over the basket is a colorful sash with intricate beadwork.

PHOTO ACKNOWLEDGMENTS:
The images in this book are used with the permission of: © Raymond Bial, pp. 1, 3, 4, 5, 7, 12, 20, 28, 34, 42; Peabody Museum, Harvard University, 41-72-10/27, p. 6; © Marilyn "Angel" Wynn/Nativestock.com, pp. 9, 10, 11, 16; © MPI/Getty Images, pp. 13, 15, 30, 31; © Burstein Collection/CORBIS, p. 14; © Choctaw Nation of Oklahoma, pp. 17, 46, 47; National Anthropological Archives, Smithsonian Institution/ BAE GN 01102D, p. 18; Library of Congress, pp. 21 (LC-USZ62-354), 26 (LC-USZ62-78307), 27, 29 (LC-USZ62-3081), 32, 36 (LC-DIG-ggbain-24179), 37 (LC-DIG-cwpb-01550), 38 (LC-USZ62-13992), 39 (LC-USZ62-116354), 40 (LC-USZ62-58502); © Michael Maslan Historic Photographs/CORBIS, p. 22; Harold R. Walters/American Museum of Natural History (3376004), p. 23; Courtesy of The Museum of Mobile, p. 24; © North Wind Picture Archives, p. 25; Mississippi Department of Archives and History, p. 33; Woolaroc Museum, Bartlesville, OK, p. 35; © Bettmann/CORBIS, p. 45; © AP/Wide World Photos, pp. 48, 49.

Cover: © Raymond Bial

Lerner Publications Company
A division of Lerner Publishing Group
241 First Avenue North
Minneapolis, MN 55401 U.S.A.

Website address: www.lernerbooks.com

Library of Congress Cataloging-in-Publication Data

Sonneborn, Liz.
    The Choctaws / by Liz Sonneborn.
        p.    cm. — (Native American histories)
    Includes bibliographical references and index.
    ISBN-13: 978-0-8225-5911-5 (lib. bdg. : alk. paper)
    ISBN-10: 0-8225-5911-0 (lib. bdg. : alk. paper)
        1. Choctaw Indians—History—Juvenile literature. 2. Choctaw Indians—Social life and customs—Juvenile literature. I. Title. II. Series.
    E99.C8S75 2007
    976.004'97387—dc22                                                005032206

Manufactured in the United States of America
1 2 3 4 5 6 – DP – 12 11 10 09 08 07

# CONTENTS

# CHAPTER 1

# FROM NANIH WAIYA

**A LARGE MOUND STANDS IN THE STATE OF MISSISSIPPI.** The mound is called Nanih Waiya. Long ago, the Great Spirit created people within Nanih Waiya. These people then crawled through a hole in the ground and reached the surface of the earth. They settled there and did well.

This tale is one story the Choctaw Indians tell about their past. The Choctaws once had a large homeland in the southeastern United States. Their lands included much of Mississippi. They also lived in parts of Alabama, Georgia, and Louisiana. The Choctaws were one of the largest and most powerful Native American tribes in the region.

## IN A CHOCTAW VILLAGE

Choctaw territory was a land of rolling hills. Much of it was covered with thick forests and flowing rivers. The climate was mild with plenty of rain.

Nanih Waiya mound *(below)* is important to the Choctaw peoples. Some believe it is the birthplace of all Choctaws.

The Choctaws lived in about fifty villages. Some were small. They had fewer than one hundred people. Others were large. They might house up to one thousand.

The villages were built near rivers. The soil there was moist and sandy. It was easy to farm with simple tools. The Choctaws could work the land with digging sticks. They used these sticks to poke holes in the ground. Then they planted seeds in the holes.

This painting shows Choctaws at work in their village. The Choctaws lived in about fifty villages.

A Mississippian house had strong mud walls and a grass roof. The Choctaws built their houses based on designs used by their ancestors, the Mississippians.

Many houses stood in each village. In fact, each family had two. One was for the winter. The other was for the summer. To make a house, the family first built a wooden frame. They made the frame of the house with standing posts. The builders buried one end of the posts in the ground. Then they packed mud between the posts. Grass or cane—tough, hollow plant stems—formed the roof.

## FARMING THE LAND

Near each family's home was a field. Men cleared the land and helped with the planting. But women were responsible for tending the crops. The women also gathered wild plant foods, such as nuts and berries.

## CLOTHING AND ORNAMENTS

The Choctaws wore clothing made of deerskin. When it was cold, people wore fur robes. Both men and women loved to dress up in jewelry and ornaments. They wore necklaces, earrings, and bracelets made of shell. Important men also tattooed their faces and bodies. Some men had flattened foreheads. The Choctaws thought this made them very good-looking. When these men were infants, their parents tied a piece of wood or a bag of sand to their forehead. Since a baby's skull is soft, this flattened their heads for life.

These modern Choctaw girls are wearing colorful and decorated formal clothes. Choctaw children of the past would have worn clothes similar to these for ceremonies or other special occasions. They wore everyday clothes to work in the fields.

Children often helped out. Their most important job was watching over the fields. They looked for birds or small animals that tried to eat the sprouting plants. When the children saw one, they shouted and shooed it away.

The Choctaws grew and ate corn, beans, and squash. These main crops were known as the "Three Sisters." Corn was the most important of the three. It was used in many dishes.

The Choctaws grew beans, squash, pumpkins, and melons. But their most important crop was corn. Women cooked many corn dishes. One of the Choctaws' favorites was *bunaha*. Women made these big dumplings from pounded cornmeal and boiled beans. They wrapped the dumplings in corn husks. Then they steamed them.

## HUNTING AND FISHING

After the harvest, men headed to the forests. There, they hunted deer, bears, and some smaller animals. They used bows and arrows to hunt.

Boys hunted smaller animals with blowguns made of cane. Blowing hard into the hollow cane, they shot cane darts at their prey.

Men also caught fish. Fishermen traveled rivers in dugout canoes carved from logs. Men also used dugouts to go on trading trips.

Late winter was sometimes a difficult time for the Choctaws. If their harvest was small or the hunt was poor, they did not have enough to eat. But usually, by working together, they had plenty of food until spring.

A traditional cane blowgun lies next to wooden darts padded with thistle down tails. Choctaw blowguns could be short or as long as 7 feet (2 meters).

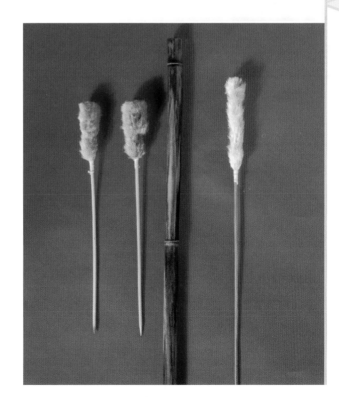

# CHAPTER 2

# LEADING THE PEOPLE

## THE CHOCTAWS LOOKED TO CHIEFS FOR LEADERSHIP. Each village had its own chief. Chiefs were usually warriors who had fought well in battle. They held their post only as long as their followers trusted them. Chiefs could be replaced if they did not do a good job.

Village councils helped chiefs make decisions. These councils were made up of older men. They were known for their wisdom.

The Choctaw villages were divided into three groups, or districts. For matters affecting the entire tribe, the three district chiefs met and reached decisions together. No single chief spoke for all the Choctaws.

This painting shows how a village chief and council might have held a meeting. Each Choctaw village had a chief too. A council of elders advised the chief and helped make decisions.

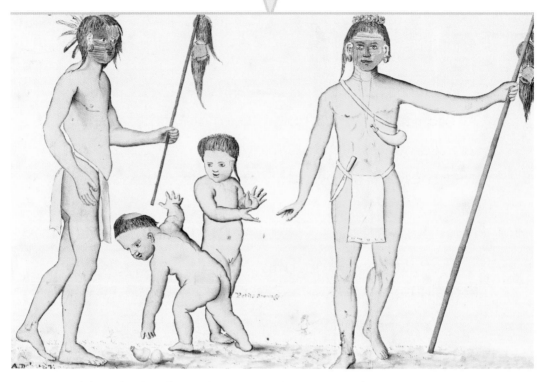

This painting from the 1700s shows two Choctaw warriors.
The men are armed with knives and lances.

## GOING TO WAR

Councils sometimes decided to go to war when
enemies invaded their land. Young men were glad
to fight the Choctaws' enemies. By proving
themselves in war, they earned the respect of their
tribe members.

Choctaw warriors spent days preparing for
battle. They rubbed their bodies with herbs. They
believed the herbs would give them strength and
courage. Warriors also danced a special war dance.

All the Choctaws celebrated a victory in battle. As the warriors returned to their village, they shouted out a victory cry. Everyone came out to greet them. Together, they danced in celebration.

## PLAYING STICKBALL

The Choctaws did not always settle conflicts through battle. When two Choctaw villages had a disagreement, they often settled it by playing a game called *ishtaboli*, or stickball. That is why the Choctaws called stickball the "little brother of war."

In this 1835 painting, hundreds of Choctaw players compete during a game of ishtaboli. Men and women played the game.

This Choctaw stickball player holds two netted sticks to catch and throw the game ball. In the past, the Choctaws often played ishtaboli to settle disputes between families or villages.

Players held a stick in each hand. Each stick had a small net on one end. Using the sticks, players carried a leather ball across a field. A goal made of a wooden pole stood at each end of the field. A player scored one point by hitting the pole with the ball.

On the day of the game, hundreds of men took the field. The only rule was that they could not touch the ball with their hands. But just about everything else was allowed. They could bump into other players or even trip them. Not surprisingly, people often got hurt.

The Choctaw people believed that spirit beings determined the winner. Before the game, religious leaders prayed and held ceremonies. They asked the spirit beings to help their side win.

A Choctaw man wears traditional clothing and performs a dance. In the past, Choctaw men and women performed similar dances before stickball games. The dances asked the spirits to help their teams win.

# THE WORLD OF THE SPIRITS

The Choctaws believed spirits controlled everything in the world. Spirits could be good or evil. To protect themselves from evil spirits, people carried charms.

Healers held rituals to drive the bad spirits away. They also treated illness with medicines made from herbs and roots. Healers were usually men, but some women were also trained in medicine.

A Choctaw burial platform from about 1775. Burial of the dead was an important part of Choctaw spiritual life.

## A CHOCTAW FUNERAL

The Choctaws held elaborate funeral ceremonies. When someone died, people placed the body outside on a wooden platform. Family members mourned. After six months, the dead person's family gathered at the platform. They cried and sang. The family members then buried the body. But they placed the bones in a box or basket. The family members carried the bones to the village's bone house. When the bone house became full, the Choctaws buried the bones. Sometimes they heaped a small mound of dirt over the burial site.

Together, the Choctaws performed ceremonies to please the good spirits. The most important was the Green Corn Ceremony. It was held in late summer, when the corn crop ripened. The Choctaws danced and sang to give thanks to the spirits for this great gift.

# CHAPTER 3
# OUTSIDERS ARRIVE

**THE CHOCTAWS WERE NOT THE ONLY INDIANS IN THE SOUTHEAST.** Several large tribes lived nearby. The Creek lived to the east. The Chickasaw lived to the north. The Choctaws rarely fought with these groups.

## MEETING EUROPEANS

In the 1540s, another group of people came to the Southeast. They were Spanish soldiers led by Hernando de Soto. De Soto came looking for gold. But he failed to find any riches. While in the Southeast, he probably came upon some Choctaw people.

Spanish explorer Hernando de Soto *(right)* explored much of what is now Florida and the southeast United States. His search for gold and other riches took him to the Choctaw homeland.

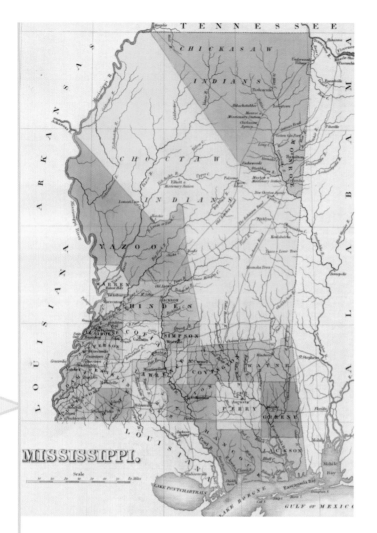

This map shows the Choctaw homeland *(large yellow area)* in what is now the state of Mississippi. English and French explorers started arriving at the Choctaw homeland in the 1600s.

By the late 1600s, however, the Choctaws had definitely met other Europeans. Some were from France. Others were from Great Britain. The French and the British came to trade. The Choctaws and other Indians offered them deerskins and corn. In exchange, these foreigners gave them guns, knives, axes, cooking pots, and other metal objects.

Europeans also brought illness to the Choctaws. From traders, the Choctaws caught diseases, such as smallpox and measles. Thousands of tribe members died.

## ALLIES OF THE FRENCH

The French and the British were enemies. Both wanted the Indian trade all to themselves. Each group tried to drive the other out of the Southeast. They often asked the Indians they traded with to help them fight.

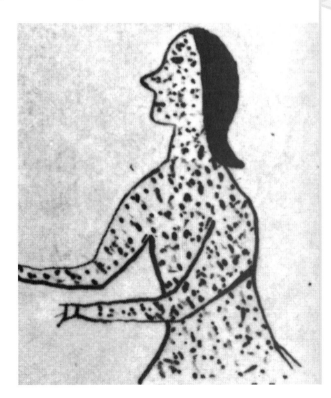

This drawing shows a Native American man sick with the measles. Europeans unknowingly brought the measles and other illnesses to America.

In 1702, the leaders of the three Choctaw districts met with Henri de Tonti, a French trader. The Choctaws agreed to be allies of the French, since they needed French trade goods.

The British became angry. In 1711, they convinced their Indian friends to attack the Choctaws. The British led a force of thirteen hundred Creeks and two hundred Chickasaws into Choctaw territory. The army killed about two hundred Choctaws. They captured another two hundred to sell as slaves.

The Choctaws met with French trader and explorer Henri de Tonti in 1702. They agreed to become allies with the French against the British.

The French and British asked other Native Americans to join them in their battles for territory. The Choctaws fought in many battles alongside the French.

The French also drew the Choctaws into their wars. They often asked the Choctaws to fight Indians who supported the British. In the 1730s, the Choctaws fought two major wars against the Chickasaw. But they failed to defeat this rival tribe.

## DEALING WITH AMERICANS

In 1763, the British won their war with the French. The French had to leave the Southeast. The Choctaws lost their closest European supporters.

Soon after, British settlers fought the American Revolution (1775–1783). By winning the war, they gained their independence from Great Britain. They then referred to themselves as Americans. They called their new country the United States of America.

The British army *(left)* surrenders to the Americans in 1781. A new country was born with the victory—the United States.

In 1790, George Washington wrote this letter to the Choctaw Nation. In the letter, he calls the Choctaws brothers and promises the United States will live in peace with them.

In 1786, the Choctaws signed a written agreement called a treaty with the United States. The treaty established peace and friendship between the two nations. It set the eastern boundary of Choctaw territory and gave the United States the right to build trading posts on Choctaw lands. It also gave the tribe the protection of the U.S. Army. The tribe supported the Americans. But many Choctaws wondered if they could truly trust them.

# CHAPTER 4

# FIGHTING FOR THE HOMELAND

**WITH EACH YEAR, MORE AMERICANS CAME TO CHOCTAW LANDS.** Many were traders. Others were travelers on the Natchez Trace. This road cut right through Choctaw territory.

Beginning in 1819, missionaries came to live among the Choctaws. These people wanted to teach the tribe about the Christian religion. They also built schools where Choctaw children learned to read and write English.

Life began to change for the Choctaws. They adopted some American ways. But they did not want to be Americans. The United States said the Choctaw lands were within its borders. But the Choctaws insisted they lived in their own nation.

A missionary talks to Native Americans during the 1800s.
In 1819, missionaries came to the Choctaw Nation.

Many Choctaws lived in temporary houses during the 1800s. Choctaws had to move a lot after signing treaties that gave away more and more of their homeland.

## LOSING TERRITORY

In the early 1800s, the Choctaws signed several more treaties with the United States. In them, the tribe gave away some of its territory.

But the United States wanted even more Choctaw land. In 1820, the Choctaws agreed to give up most of their territory in Mississippi. In exchange, they received 13 million acres

(5 million hectares) to the west. The land was in Indian Territory. Later, it became Oklahoma.

A few Choctaws moved to Indian Territory. But most of them stayed in Mississippi. U.S. government officials were not pleased. They wanted all the Choctaws to move west.

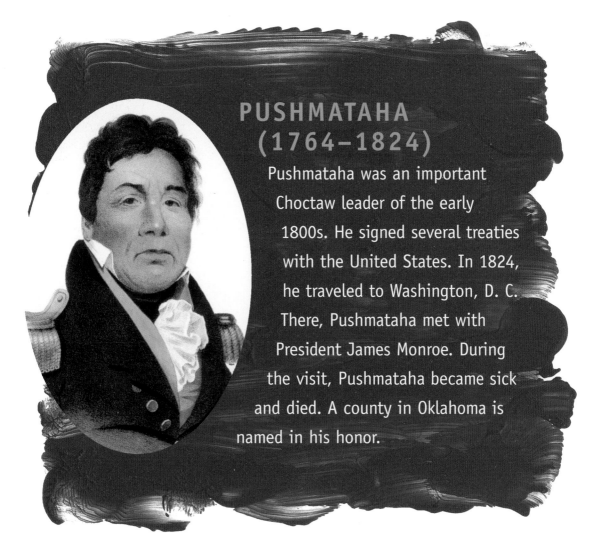

## PUSHMATAHA (1764–1824)

Pushmataha was an important Choctaw leader of the early 1800s. He signed several treaties with the United States. In 1824, he traveled to Washington, D. C. There, Pushmataha met with President James Monroe. During the visit, Pushmataha became sick and died. A county in Oklahoma is named in his honor.

This U.S. document is part of the 1830 Treaty of Dancing Rabbit Creek. The treaty asks Choctaws to give up their homeland for land in Indian Territory.

# THE TREATY OF DANCING RABBIT CREEK

In 1830, Choctaw leaders met with U.S. officials at Dancing Rabbit Creek. The officials wanted the Choctaws to agree to move west. Most Choctaw leaders refused and left the meeting.

But a few leaders stayed behind. They signed a treaty. It promised that the Choctaw tribe would head west. Individual Choctaws could choose to stay in the East—but only if they agreed to live by Mississippi law.

The treaty upset many Choctaw people. They were angry at the leaders who signed it. Some said those leaders had taken money from the Americans in exchange for signing the treaty.

Within five years, about fourteen thousand Choctaws moved west. About five thousand stayed and became citizens of Mississippi. From then on, the Choctaws were a divided people.

Choctaw chief Mushulatubbee *(right)* was one of the Choctaw leaders who signed removal treaties with the United States. He believed the treaties were best for his people. Other Choctaws strongly disagreed with him. They refused to leave their homeland.

# CHAPTER 5

# INTO THE WEST

**MOST OF THE CHOCTAWS HEADED WEST DURING THE WINTER OF 1831.** Others followed during the next two years. Some Choctaws went to Indian Territory on steamboats. But many more traveled there on foot. They often did not have enough food or blankets for everyone. Many became sick, walking day after day in the cold winter weather. About twenty-five hundred Choctaws died on the journey. It became known as the Trail of Tears.

# REBUILDING THEIR WORLD

Slowly, the Choctaws rebuilt their lives in the West. They built farms along riverbeds. They cut down trees and constructed houses.

The Choctaws formed a new government. The tribe also built schools. Missionaries who came west with the Choctaws helped them. These missionaries established Christian churches in the new Choctaw Nation.

This painting shows the Cherokees' journey to Indian Territory, or the Trail of Tears. Like the Choctaws, they were forced to leave their homeland and move west. Many died on these journeys.

Native Americans harvest wheat in Indian Territory during the 1800s. The Choctaws and many other Native Americans from the Southeast had to plant different crops when they moved to the West.

To survive in the West, the Choctaws changed some of their ways. For instance, they started growing wheat. It grew better than corn did in their new homeland. They also spent less time farming and more time raising livestock. Their western territory had many grassy areas where these animals could graze.

## THE CIVIL WAR

The western Choctaws started to thrive. But in 1861, they faced a new problem. The United States was caught up in a civil war over the question of slavery. Some Southerners kept slaves. Many people in the North were against slavery. The states in the North fought the states in the South. Each side wanted the Choctaws' support.

Wounded Native American soldiers rest during the Civil War (1861–1865). The Choctaws and other Indians were asked to take sides in the war.

This drawing from 1864 shows soldiers on a cattle raid. During the Civil War, raiders took horses, cattle, and grain from the Choctaws and other people.

The Choctaws sided with the South. Many tribespeople still had ties to the area. Also, some Choctaws were slave owners. They did not want the North to outlaw slavery.

The Choctaw people suffered during the war. Raiders roamed through their lands, stealing crops and livestock. After the North won, the United States wanted to punish the Choctaws for supporting the South. Government officials made the Choctaw leaders give up much of their western territory.

# A CHANGING NATION

After the war, the Choctaws had more challenges. Trains began traveling through Indian Territory. They brought even more non-Indian settlers to the Choctaw Nation. These settlers did not want to obey Choctaw leaders. They wanted the Choctaw Nation to become part of the United States.

In the late 1800s, U. S. officials came up with a plan. They wanted to divide the Choctaw Nation into allotments. These were small plots of land.

The Transcontinental Railroad joined the East and the West of the United States in 1869. Trains brought settlers to the Indian Territory and to the Choctaw Nation.

Each allotment would belong to a single family. Once every family had an allotment, the officials wanted to dissolve the Choctaw government.

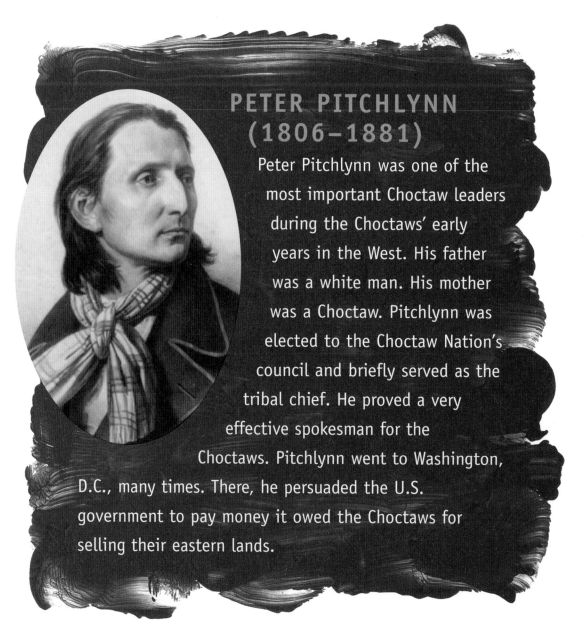

## PETER PITCHLYNN (1806–1881)

Peter Pitchlynn was one of the most important Choctaw leaders during the Choctaws' early years in the West. His father was a white man. His mother was a Choctaw. Pitchlynn was elected to the Choctaw Nation's council and briefly served as the tribal chief. He proved a very effective spokesman for the Choctaws. Pitchlynn went to Washington, D.C., many times. There, he persuaded the U.S. government to pay money it owed the Choctaws for selling their eastern lands.

The Choctaws fought against allotment. They wanted to keep their own nation and govern it as they chose. But U.S. officials ignored their wishes. In 1907, the Choctaw Nation became part of the new state of Oklahoma.

## THE CHOCTAWS OF ARDMORE

In the early 1900s, more than four hundred Mississippi Choctaws headed to Indian Territory. These people wanted to claim an allotment in western Choctaw territory. For most, the trip was paid for by the U.S. government. But about forty were victims of a trick planned by crooks. The crooks promised to pay the Choctaws' way west. But once they were there, the crooks planned to steal the Choctaws' allotments and then sell the Choctaws as slaves. U.S. officials found out about the plot and saved the Choctaws. They settled in the town of Ardmore. About nine hundred Choctaws still live in Ardmore, Oklahoma.

## CHAPTER 6

# THE MODERN-DAY CHOCTAWS

**THE EARLY 1900S WERE A DIFFICULT TIME FOR THE CHOCTAWS.** In both the East and the West, they struggled to get by. Some worked as farmers or ranchers. Others found jobs in timber and mining companies.

Most Choctaws continued to live in Oklahoma and Mississippi. But a few Choctaws established communities in other areas. Many of these people settled in Louisiana and Texas.

## THE JENA BAND

In 1850, a group of eastern Choctaws boarded a boat bound for Indian Territory. But five families got off before they got there. These Choctaws settled in central Louisiana. For many years, they kept to themselves. They lived much as their ancestors had, with little contact with outsiders. In 1995, the United States recognized them as a tribe. They are called the Jena Band of Choctaw Indians. The Jena Band has about 240 members.

In search of work, other Choctaws moved to cities. But they tried to keep in touch with old friends and relatives. When they could, they visited Choctaw communities. There, they might play a game of stickball or attend a church service held in the Choctaw language.

## JOSEPH OKLAHOMBI (D. 1960)

Joseph Oklahombi was a famous Choctaw soldier in World War I (1914–1918). He and other Choctaw soldiers were the original "Code Talkers." They used their native Choctaw to send messages from one group of soldiers to another. The Germans were never able to break the code.

Joseph also captured three machine-gun nests and 171 German soldiers by himself. For his bravery, he was awarded the Croix de Guerre by the French government and the Silver Star by the U.S. government.

This is the official seal of the Choctaws of Oklahoma. The calumet, or pipe, stands for tradition. The bow means strength, and the three arrows stand for three great Choctaw chiefs.

## THE CHOCTAW NATION OF OKLAHOMA

In the 1930s, the Choctaws in Oklahoma formed a new government. Representatives from the Choctaw Nation met in 1934. They established an advisory council. In 1948, some Choctaws elected a chief, Harry J. W. Belvin.

Modern-day Oklahoma Choctaws also elect a chief. With the council, the chief governs the tribe's 127,000 members. These officials oversee many programs to help improve the Choctaws' lives. The Choctaw government runs a hospital and many clinics. It also provides needy tribe members with housing and child care.

The Choctaw Nation Hospital *(below)* is in Talihina, Oklahoma. The hospital serves Choctaws and other Native Americans.

Women wait to perform a traditional Choctaw dance at the annual Labor Day Festival in Durant, Oklahoma. The Choctaws preserve their culture through tribal events such as this festival.

The tribal government employs many people. It operates several businesses. They include bingo parlors, travel centers, a cattle ranch, and other tribal operations.

Each year, the Oklahoma Choctaws also host the Choctaw Nation Labor Day Festival. There, visitors can learn about traditional Choctaw culture. They can see displays of baskets and other crafts or watch stickball games and Choctaw dances.

## THE MISSISSIPPI BAND OF CHOCTAW INDIANS

In recent years, the Mississippi Choctaws have prospered. Before 1944, most of these Choctaws had no official homeland. But in that year, the United States granted them several reservations. (A reservation is land set aside for a particular Indian group.) Seven Choctaw communities exist in the state. About nine thousand people are enrolled in the Mississippi Choctaw band.

Chief Phillip Martin gives a speech on tradition and the future. He and a council lead the Mississippi Choctaw band.

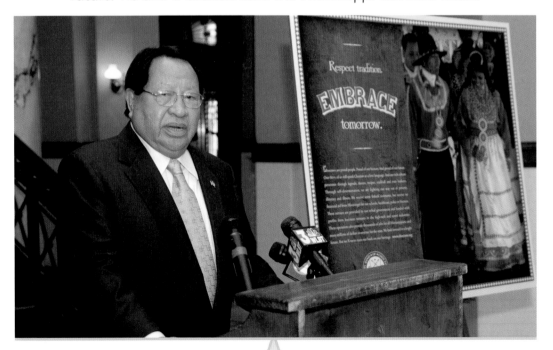

The Choctaws of Mississippi run several businesses, including the Silver Star casino *(above)*. These businesses bring jobs and money to the Choctaw people and their reservations.

Like their Oklahoma relatives, the Mississippi Choctaws have a chief and a tribal council. They work to provide educational programs and health care for their people. The Mississippi Choctaws also own many businesses, including factories and a golf course. They run several profitable resort casinos, where visitors come to gamble.

## NOTEWORTHY CHOCTAWS

Many modern-day Choctaws have excelled in their fields. They include historians Clara Sue Kidwell and Devon Mihesuah, archaeologists Dorothy Lippert and Joe Watkins, and artists Gary White Deer and Valjean Hessing, to name a few.

Every July, visitors flock to the annual Choctaw Indian Fair. It is one of the biggest festivals in the Southeast. People come to see Choctaw dancing and watch famous country music acts perform. One popular event at the fair is a beauty pageant. The winner is crowned that year's Choctaw princess.

Since the 1830s, the Choctaws in Mississippi and Oklahoma have lived apart. But they still share their pride in being Choctaw. No matter where they live, the Choctaws celebrate their past and future as the children of Nanih Waiya.

# THE CHOCTAW LANGUAGE

The Choctaws have worked hard to keep the Choctaw language alive. In both Oklahoma and Mississippi, tribe members hold classes to make sure children learn to speak Choctaw. The Oklahoma Choctaws even offer classes over the Internet.

You can use the chart below to learn how to count to ten in Choctaw.

| English Word | Choctaw Word | Pronunciation |
| --- | --- | --- |
| one | achafi | ah-chuh-fee |
| two | tuklo | too-kloh |
| three | tuchina | too-chee-nah |
| four | ushta | oosh-tah |
| five | talapi | tah-lah-pee |
| six | hannali | hah-nah-lee |
| seven | untuklo | oon-too-kloh |
| eight | untuchina | oon-too-chee-nah |
| nine | chakali | chah-kah-lee |
| ten | pokoli | poh-koh-lee |

# PLACES TO VISIT

**Choctaw Indian Fair**

*Choctaw, MS*

(601) 656-5251

The Mississippi Band of Choctaw Indians has held this annual regional fair since 1949. It features stickball games, craft displays, dance contests, and country music concerts.

**Choctaw National Historical Museum**

*Route 1*

*Box 105AAA*

*Tuskahoma, OK 74574*

(918) 569-4465

This museum is housed in a building that was once the capitol of the Choctaw Nation. The collection presents the tribe's history through objects, paintings, and photographs.

**Choctaw Nation Labor Day Festival**

*Choctaw Nation*

*Tuskahoma, OK*

(580) 924-8280

Since 1884, Choctaws have hosted this festival over Labor Day weekend. Visitors can eat traditional Choctaw food, watch stickball games, and attend dance performances.

**Chucalissa Museum**

*1987 Indian Village Drive*

*Memphis, TN 38109*

(901) 785-3160

http://www.chucalissa.org

This museum features a reconstruction of a Choctaw village from the 1400s.

# GLOSSARY

**allotment:** a plot of land that is given to a person or group

**ally:** a nation or group that pledges support to another nation or group

**American Indian:** anyone native to North or South America, or a person descended from these natives. American Indians are also called Native Americans.

**band:** a small group of Native American families who share the same language, customs, and religious beliefs. Bands are smaller than tribes.

**civil war:** a war fought between groups of people within the same country

**ishtaboli:** a game of stickball. Players use netted sticks to carry and throw a game ball. They score by hitting a wooden post (goal) with the ball.

**missionaries:** people who try to persuade others to adopt their religion

**Nanih Waiya:** a mound of earth in central Mississippi. Traditional stories say that the Choctaws come from this place.

**official:** a person employed by a government

**reservation:** an area of land set aside by the U.S. government for a particular American Indian group

**treaty:** a written agreement between two or more nations or groups

**tribe:** a group of American Indians who share the same language, customs, and religious beliefs

# FURTHER READING

Bial, Raymond. *The Choctaw*. New York: Benchmark Books, 2003.

Harrell, Beatrice Orcutt. *Longwalker's Journey: A Novel of the Choctaw Trail of Tears*. New York: Dial Books for Young Readers, 1999.

McKee, Jesse O. *The Choctaw*. New York: Chelsea House Publishers, 1990.

Tingle, Tim. *Walking the Choctaw Road: Stories from Red People Memory*. El Paso, TX: Cinco Puntos Press, 2003.

# WEBSITES

**Choctaw Nation of Oklahoma**
http://www.choctawnation.com
This site contains information about the history, culture, and contemporary life of the Oklahoma Choctaws.

**Jena Band of Choctaw Indians**
http://www.jenachoctaw.org
The official site of the Jena Band describes various tribal government programs benefiting this branch of the Choctaws.

**Mississippi Band of Choctaw Indians**
http://www.choctaw.org
The Mississippi Band's website records the past and present of the Choctaws in the East.

# SELECTED BIBLIOGRAPHY

Byington, Cyrus. *A Dictionary of the Choctaw Language*. Reprint, 1915. Brighton, MI: Native American Book Publishers, 1990.

Davis, Mary B., ed. *Native America in the Twentieth Century*. New York: Garland Publishing, 1996.

Debo, Angie. *The Rise and Fall of the Choctaw Republic*. 2nd ed. Norman, OK: University of Oklahoma Press, 1961.

Fogelson, Raymond, ed. *Handbook of North American Indians: The Southeast*. Vol. 14. Washington, DC: Smithsonian Institution Press, 2004.

Hoxie, Frederick E., ed. *Encyclopedia of North American Indians*. Boston: Houghton Mifflin, 1996.

Waldman, Carl. *Biographical Dictionary of American Indian History to 1900*. Rev. ed. New York: Facts On File, 2001.

———. *Encyclopedia of Native American Tribes*. Rev. ed. New York: Facts On File, 1999.

# INDEX